How to Solve These M

Here is some important advice to give anyone trying to solve one of these mysteries:

- Read carefully and keep in mind that everything you read is a true statement. If someone says he/she has have never stolen something, then that means he/she has never stolen something in his/her entire life.
- Proving a suspect's innocence is often necessary to finding the thief. Some mysteries require you to figure out which of the suspects are innocent to then figure out which of the suspects is the thief.
- When you read clues describing one of the suspects or the thief, compare that information to the pictures. Some clues are a combination of text and a picture or pictures.
- Pay close attention to what is fact and what is opinion. In most cases, someone's opinion is not relevant to solving the case.
- Beware of vague statements. If someone says something that isn't clear, then don't assume or guess the meaning.
- Make notes when you believe you have found evidence of innocence or guilt. There is a lot of detail in the mystery, and often, innocence or guilt is the result of synthesizing different pieces of evidence.
- These mysteries are not easy, but don't give up! It may help to take a break and come back to it later.

Hints

If you absolutely, positively need to give someone a hint, use part of an answer for a hint.

Read the mystery below to find evidence to identify the innocent and guilty suspects. Remember, the story and suspects' statements are true.

The Car Thief

[1]Today, police in the City of Reedsport arrested one of the four boys shown below for stealing Tommy Porter's car. [2]The theft took place on April 12, of this year between 1 p.m. and 2 p.m. [3]Porter had his car stolen from outside a restaurant in Reedsport where he was eating lunch. [4]After lunch, Porter returned to where he had parked his car, but the car was gone. [5]A witness to the theft said he saw a lone young man break into and drive away in the car just minutes earlier. [6]The witness said the thief was six feet or slightly taller with blond or brownish hair, tanned or kind of darkish skin, some facial hair, and dark pants. [7]The arrest was made in the evening on the day of the theft, and the thief confessed to the crime.

Bill Lucero

[8]I was in Reedsport on the morning of the 12th by myself but I left town before 2 p.m.

Jake Smith

[9]I ate lunch in Reedsport that day, but I did not get into town before 2 p.m.

Trey Woods

[10]I was in Reedsport the week of the 12th but was always with two friends. [11]All of us are about six feet tall.

Ben Daily

[12]On the 12th, I ate lunch before noon in Reedsport but left town before 2 p.m.

Critical Thinking Detective™

Book 1

Critical Thinking Detective™ series is available in print or eBook form.

Beginning • Book 1

Written by
Michael Baker

Edited by
Patricia Gray

Graphic Design by
Scott Slyter

THE CRITICAL THINKING CO.™
www.CriticalThinking.com
Phone: 800-458-4849 • Fax: 541-756-1758
1991 Sherman Ave., Suite 200 • North Bend • OR 97459
ISBN 978-1-60144-897-2

Printed in the United States of America by Edwards Brothers Malloy, Inc., Ann Arbor, MI (Feb. 2017)

Table of Contents

About This Book

This book offers a collection of fun, easy-to-use detective mysteries for Grades 4 – 12+. That is a wide grade range, but anyone who can carefully read these mysteries and is willing to study the evidence can solve them. They are not solved through tricky logic or advanced math concepts.

Some mysteries may be more challenging for younger students, but teachers and parents can always provide hints if absolutely needed. The mysteries develop critical thinking skills by requiring students to read carefully and analyze and synthesize information to guide their decision-making. The mysteries also develop observation skills, reading comprehension, deductive and inductive thinking skills. The ability to identify and evaluate evidence is the very heart of critical thinking.

For a more lesson-based approach to teach critical thinking, we recommend *The Basics of Critical Thinking* (Grades 4 – 9) and *Practical Critical Thinking* (Grades 9 – 12+).

The Innocent

Use complete sentences and sentence numbers to describe the best evidence for your conclusions.

______________________________ (suspect name)

______________________________ (suspect name)

______________________________ (suspect name)

The Car Thief

______________________________ (suspect name)

Read the mystery below to find evidence to identify the innocent and guilty suspects. Remember, the story and suspects' statements are true.

The Lunch Money Thief

[1]Today, police in the City of Watsonville arrested one of the four students shown below for stealing lunch money from the Watsonville High School cafeteria. [2]The lunch money, a five-dollar bill, belonged to Olga Clemens. [3]The theft took place on Friday, November 11, between 11:30 a.m. and 12:30 p.m. [4]All four suspects were in the cafeteria when Olga Clemens put the money down on the counter and then walked a few feet away to look at the salads. [5]When she returned, the money was gone, and the suspects below were in line either in front or behind her. [6]Clemens then took the four girls to the principal's office until the police arrived.

[7]In the office, each of the suspects gave a statement to the principal. [8]Edwards said she left the cafeteria with less than five dollars. [9]Morgan said she had her own money and didn't need to steal Clemens's money. [10]Mott said she entered the cafeteria with only a twenty-dollar bill. [11]Ueberrhein said that she left the counter with the same amount of money she had when she entered the cafeteria.

[12]When the police arrived just after 12:30, the principal told them what the suspects had told her, and then they heard the suspects' statements below. [13]After gathering all this information, the police asked one of the suspects additional questions, and then the girl confessed to the crime and handed them the stolen money.

Deanna Edwards
[14]I was really hungry, so I had a big lunch today, but I paid for it with money in my pocket.

Jodi Morgan
[15]I never thought Clemens was a very nice person, so I've never had anything to do with her.

Jane Mott
[16]I left the cafeteria with 15 dollars after spending 5 dollars on my lunch. [17]I spent my own money in the cafeteria and never had someone else's.

Susan Ueberrhein
[18]I decided I didn't like what they were serving, so I never bought anything or spent any money.

The Innocent

Use complete sentences and sentence numbers to describe the best evidence for your conclusions.

______________________________ (suspect name)

______________________________ (suspect name)

______________________________ (suspect name)

The Lunch Money Thief

______________________________ (suspect name)

Read the mystery below to find evidence to identify the innocent and guilty suspects. Remember, the story and suspects' statements are true.

The Chicken Breast Thief

[1]On Sunday, October 4, a chicken breast was taken off a table next to a barbeque in the Gray family's backyard. [2]At the time of the theft, the Grays and a few of their dinner guests were chatting inside the Gray's house. [3]A few of the people at the dinner party saw a cat around the Gray's house at the time of theft and four of them even saw the chicken breast in a cat's mouth as it left the yard. [4]Their statements are listed below.

[5]After the theft, the Grays went to the yard to find and gather their two cats. [6]Terry McDonald, their only neighbor with cats, also left to search for his two cats to bring them to the Gray's house, so they could all work together to identify the chicken breast thief.

Nick Workhoven
[7]I saw the cat leaving the backyard with the chicken breast in his mouth. [8]He was gray or black with yellow or gold eyes. [9] His tail was kind of short and at least one of his front legs was a lighter gray than the back of his ears.

Kathy Litts
[10]I saw a cat in the front yard and he was gray or black and had rounded ears. [11]His eyes were yellow or gold with black pupils. [12]His head was big and round.

Scott Jacobsen
[13]I saw a gray cat with a light gray neck and yellow or gold eyes leaving the backyard with the chicken breast in his mouth.

Ellie Jacobsen
[14]I saw the thief jump down from the table with the chicken breast in his mouth. [15]He was black or gray with two light gray legs.

Richard Litts
[16]I saw the cat running with the chicken breast. [17]He was gray or black with yellow or gold eyes and pointed ears.

[18]After hearing from the witnesses, Terry McDonald announced he knew who the thief was and looked into the cat's mouth and saw pieces of the barbequed chicken breast in his teeth. [19]The dinner guests all laughed and agreed that the thief should not get his normal canned food tonight, since he had already had his dinner.

The Innocent

Use complete sentences and sentence numbers to describe the best evidence for your conclusions.

______________________________ (suspect name)

____

____

____

____

______________________________ (suspect name)

____

____

____

____

______________________________ (suspect name)

____

____

____

____

The Chicken Breast Thief

______________________________ (suspect name)

____

____

____

____

Read the mystery below to find evidence to identify the innocent and guilty suspects. Remember, the story and suspects' statements are true.

The Necklace Thief

[1]Today, police in the City of Florence arrested one of the four women shown below for stealing a necklace from Ortega's Jewelry Store. [2]The necklace was made of blue and green gems on a gold chain. [3]The theft took place on Wednesday, July 15, between 3 p.m. and 5 p.m. [4]All four suspects were in the store during the time of the theft and remained in the store until the police solved the crime.

[5]Collier said everything in the store was overpriced. [6]Porter knows Zomerschoe and said she didn't think that Zomerschoe would ever steal anything. [7]The lone witness told police the thief had difficulty walking. [8]He also said the thief was easily more than fifty years old and wore something kind of orange or red in color. [9]He didn't see the thief's face but heard her asking the owner a question about the necklace before the theft. [10]The witness said the thief had wavy or curly hair. [11]After listening to all four suspect statements below, between 5 p.m. and 6 p.m., the police arrested one of the suspects in the store. [12]The suspect confessed to the crime, returned the necklace to the owner, and apologized to her.

Shannon Porter

[13]I picked up the necklace to look at it, but I left it on the counter before 3 p.m. and never had it again.

Terri Collier

[14]I looked at the necklace on the counter and asked the man who was helping me about it. [15]I didn't talk to anyone else until the police arrived.

Mindy Smith

[16]I bought a blue and green bracelet and was waited on by a very nice young man. [17]He was the only person I saw or talked to before 5 p.m.

Miriam Zomerschoe

[18]I didn't try on a necklace, but I talked to a woman at the counter just after 4 p.m. [19]She was the only person I talked to.

The Innocent

Use complete sentences and sentence numbers to describe the best evidence for your conclusions.

______________________________ (suspect name)

____

____

____

____

______________________________ (suspect name)

____

____

____

____

______________________________ (suspect name)

____

____

____

____

The Necklace Thief

______________________________ (suspect name)

____

____

____

____

Read the mystery below to find evidence to identify the innocent and guilty suspects. Remember, the story and suspects' statements are true.

The Bath Robe Thief

[1]Today, police in the City of Bandon arrested one of the four men shown below for stealing a bath robe from a clothing store. [2]The theft took place on Saturday, June 15, between 4 p.m. and 5 p.m. [3]All four suspects visited the store during that time. [4]The owner said he waited on and sold items to Baker and Giss. [5]Giss said he didn't see any socks in the store with a good price. [6]O'Bryan said he was not the last suspect to leave the store. [7]One witness saw the thief stuff the robe under his clothing. [8]The witness also told police that he didn't see the thief's face, but he was short. [9]Another witness to the theft said the thief wore glasses. [10]The arrest of the suspect, and his later confession, happened in the early evening the day of the theft. [11]The all blue and white robe was found in his apartment and returned to the store.

Michael Baker
[12]I bought a robe and some pants at the store. [13]I left with those items in a bag they gave me.

Darin O'Bryan
[14]The owner of the store and I are friends, and the stolen robe was never in my apartment.

John Nicolaus
[15]I left the store with only two items. [16]Both items were partly green.

Steve Giss
[17]I stopped at the store to buy some socks on the way to my house.

The Innocent

Use complete sentences and sentence numbers to describe the best evidence for your conclusions.

______________________________ (suspect name)

____

____

____

____

______________________________ (suspect name)

____

____

____

____

______________________________ (suspect name)

____

____

____

____

The Bath Robe Thief

______________________________ (suspect name)

____

____

____

____

Read the mystery below to find evidence to identify the innocent and guilty suspects. Remember, the story and suspects' statements are true.

The Big City Bicycle Thief

[1]Today at 12 p.m., the New York City Police arrested one of the suspects below for stealing a bicycle in front of a phone store between 9:30 a.m. and 11:00 a.m. [2]Police were helped by three witnesses who gave them statements about what they saw. [3]Each suspect also gave the police a statement which is listed below. [4]After weighing all the evidence, the police arrested one of the suspects. [5]The suspect later confessed, and the bicycle was found in his apartment.

Witness 1: [6]He was younger than me. [7]He had a dark mustache. [8]His shirt was open at the neck and had a white stripe.

Witness 2: [9]When he looked to see if the bike was locked, I saw that he had a large, red scar across his cheek.

Witness 3: [10]The thief had dark facial hair. [11]I'm pretty sure his shirt was blue or green.

Bob Veach
[12]I was in the city in the morning, but I walked home. [13]I was surprised when the police car pulled me over for questioning. [14]I've never ridden a bicycle.

Steve Berta
[15]I left the phone store shortly after 9:30 a.m. and went straight home and then straight to work until 5 p.m. [16]At one point on my way back home, I looked back and saw the bicycle in front of the store.

Sam Edwards
[17]I love to ride, but I rode to the area of the store and back on a bicycle.

Kent Kitchel
[18]I rode out of the city just after 10 a.m. this morning. [19]The police stopped me, and I gave them my statement.

The Innocent

Use complete sentences and sentence numbers to describe the best evidence for your conclusions.

______________________________ (suspect name)

____

____

____

____

______________________________ (suspect name)

____

____

____

____

______________________________ (suspect name)

____

____

____

____

The Big City Bicycle Thief

______________________________ (suspect name)

____

____

____

____

Read the mystery below to find evidence to identify the innocent and guilty suspects. Remember, the story and suspects' statements are true.

The Purse Thief

[1]Today, police in the City of Bandon arrested one of the four women shown below for stealing Kari Lyons' purse from the bleachers when she was watching a high school soccer game. [2]The theft took place on May 9 of this year between 1 p.m. and 2 p.m. [3]Lyons' purse was stolen between the 2nd and 3rd goals of the game. [4]After Lyons returned from buying a smoothie just before the beginning of the second half, she put her purse down next to her seat. [5]After the second half began, the 2nd goal of the game was scored and she put her phone in her purse. [6]After the 3rd goal was scored, she went to grab her phone to text a friend, and the purse had been stolen! [7]A witness saw a woman walking with Lyons' purse, which is decorated with a distinctive yellow, green, and purple ribbon. [8]The witness said the thief was dressed nicely and was not short. [9]She went on to say that the thief looked fit and had darkish hair. [10]The arrest and the thief's confession were made after the game ended with a final score of 3-1.

Bonnie Baker

[11]I was there for the first half but not the second half.

Mary O'Dell

[12]I arrived late, so I was only there for the final goal of the game.

Jacqueline Examilotis

[13]I watched the game until I left to buy a hot dog between the 1st and 2nd goals of the second half. [14]I then returned to watch the game.

Jessica Garrett

[15]I was there for the first half and part of the second half but left before the first goal of the second half was scored.

The Innocent

Use complete sentences and sentence numbers to describe the best evidence for your conclusions.

______________________________ (suspect name)

____

____

____

____

______________________________ (suspect name)

____

____

____

____

______________________________ (suspect name)

____

____

____

____

The Purse Thief

______________________________ (suspect name)

____

____

____

____

Read the mystery below to find evidence to identify the innocent and guilty suspects. Remember, the story and suspects' statements are true.

The Plant Thief

[1]Today, police in the City of Aptos arrested one of the four young men shown below for stealing a plant from Hull's Nursery. [2]The rare bonsai plant was an 80-year-old cherry tree that was only eight inches tall. [3]The theft took place on Saturday, July 11, in the morning. [4]The plant was on display five feet from the front counter that morning, and the owner noticed its empty pot just before noon. [5]All four suspects were in the store when the police arrived at 12:03 p.m. and were held at the store for questioning until the police solved the crime.

[6]Cort said he looked carefully at the tree and knew it was very valuable, but he walked away from it around 11:10 a.m. so others could look at it. [7]Wilson said he saw the plant just after 11 a.m., and it was still undisturbed in the pot. [8]The owner said the thief ripped the plant from the pot and could have damaged the roots while doing so. [9]Krauth said he always wanted a bonsai plant, but the plant was not in its pot when he went to the counter to pay for two potted ferns at 11:30 a.m. [10]Wilson said he didn't even know what a bonsai plant was when he entered the store. [11]After the police arrived at the store and heard these statements from the suspects and their testimonies below, the police asked one of them if he would agree to be searched; and then the suspect confessed and produced the plant from beneath his clothing.

Ross Wilson
[12]I know who took the plant.

Jorge Sanchez
[13]I looked at it, but I never thought of taking it. [14]I'm an old friend of Wilson.

Steve Krauth
[15]I knew it was valuable, but I didn't go near it after 11 a.m. [16]I know one of the other suspects.

Jeff Cort
[17]I finally decided to buy the plant but thought it had been sold when I saw it was no longer in the pot.

The Innocent

Use complete sentences and sentence numbers to describe the best evidence for your conclusions.

______________________________ (suspect name)

____

____

____

____

______________________________ (suspect name)

____

____

____

____

______________________________ (suspect name)

____

____

____

____

The Plant Thief

______________________________ (suspect name)

____

____

____

____

Read the mystery below to find evidence to identify the innocent and guilty suspects. Remember, the story and suspects' statements are true.

The Dog Food Thief

[1]On Monday, November 14, the Ortega family identified the dog that had been stealing their new puppy's dog food. [2]The puppy food was stolen from a bowl set out for the puppy in the backyard where he often plays. [3]All the thefts took place between the 7th and 14th of November. [4]The family identified the dog using witness's accounts and testimonies from the suspect dogs' owners. [5]The first theft was Monday, the 7th, between 2 p.m. and 4 p.m. [6]The next theft was between the late afternoon and the early evening on the 9th. [7]The final theft was Saturday morning. [8]All the thefts were the work of the same dog. [9]Mrs. Ortega said that all the dogs below live in the neighborhood and that both Pepper and Ralph have visited their house. [10]She also said that Pepper and Ralph sometimes hang out together, and her husband likes to call them the "hairy brothers." [11]Once the Ortega family identified the thief from the dog suspects below, they all agreed that the dog was beautiful, friendly, and very playful. [12]They also said the dog is still welcome in their yard, but they will have to be more careful with the puppy food so he can no longer steal it.

Ralph

[13]Ralph's owner said that Ralph is locked in his pen on some weekdays and every weekend until he gets home and lets him out in the afternoon.

Toby

[14]Toby's owner said that Toby loves the Ortega puppy but can only get to the Ortega's on Mondays, Thursdays, and Saturdays when her son lets him out of their backyard.

Shadow

[15]Shadow's owner said Shadow frequently plays with other dogs in the neighborhood except on Tuesdays when he takes her out of town to the hospital where he works.

Pepper

[16]Pepper's owner said that she had never been to the Ortega's home, but that Pepper is with her on Tuesdays and Thursdays and many afternoons.

The Innocent

Use complete sentences and sentence numbers to describe the best evidence for your conclusions.

______________________________ (suspect name)

____

____

____

____

______________________________ (suspect name)

____

____

____

____

______________________________ (suspect name)

____

____

____

____

The Dog Food Thief

______________________________ (suspect name)

____

____

____

____

Read the mystery below to find evidence to identify the innocent and guilty suspects. Remember, the story and suspects' statements are true.

The Tie Thief

[1]On Friday, November 9, two expensive ties were stolen from Jacobson's Men's Store. [2]At the time of the theft, the four suspects below were the only customers in the store with the owner. [3]All the suspects originally claimed their innocence, but after the police questioned them and took their statements, one of them was arrested and the ties were found hidden under his shirt.

[4]The ties were stolen from an island counter displaying more than a hundred different ties. [5]Once the thief was arrested, the owner exclaimed his surprise that one of his best buying customers would steal from him. [6]He said the thief is always sharply dressed when he comes into the store and usually wears blue. [7]He went on to say that he was surprised at the theft because the thief teaches logic and English.

Tyler Morgan

[8]I'm a local teacher, but I don't wear ties. [9]I know one of the other suspects. [10]I've been to the store many times, but I returned the only thing I ever bought there.

Ralph Smith

[11]One of the other suspects is a friend of mine. [12]I know who the thief is; me, my friend, or Slivkoff.

Steve Slivkoff

[13]I was shocked when the police made their arrest. [14]I only know Tedsen, we've worked at the same place and known each other a long time, but nothing he does has ever surprised me.

Don Tedsen

[15]I know two of the suspects from work. [16]One is an old friend, but the other is a teacher that I've never really talked to or communicated with. [17]My longtime friend didn't take the ties.

The Innocent

Use complete sentences and sentence numbers to describe the best evidence for your conclusions.

______________________________ (suspect name)

____

____

____

____

______________________________ (suspect name)

____

____

____

____

______________________________ (suspect name)

____

____

____

____

The Tie Thief

______________________________ (suspect name)

____

____

____

____

Read the mystery below to find evidence to identify the innocent and guilty suspects. Remember, the story and suspects' statements are true.

The Football Thief

[1]On Saturday, October 21, a football was stolen from the Baker's front yard. [2]Mr. and Mrs. Baker live on Morgan Street in Roseburg, Oregon, with their three sons. [3]The boys' football was stolen in the afternoon after 2 p.m. but before 4 p.m. [4]The Baker's next door neighbor, Tina Cohoe, was in the house at the time of the theft and told police that she saw a tall man wearing a green short-sleeved shirt walking away from the house around 4 p.m., and it looked like he wasn't wearing socks.

[5]Another neighbor said that he saw an adult male who was wearing a green shirt and carrying a jacket walking away from the Baker's house on the sidewalk in front of their yard. [6]Each of the four suspects below was walking alone on Morgan Street when they were stopped by police just after 4 p.m. on the afternoon of the crime to get their statements. [7]They were the only suspects in the investigation that led to an arrest.

[8]After weighing all the evidence from the Baker's neighbors, and the suspects' statements below, the police arrested one of the suspects and found the Baker's football behind a nearby bush next to the sidewalk. [9]After his arrest, the suspect confessed to the crime.

Norm Day

[10]I'm not a big football fan anymore, but my son plays, so the only football I've seen in the last five days is the one I gave him last Sunday.

Kyle Meizner

[11]I played football in high school until I got cut from the team as a senior. [12]I've never played or watched a football game since.

Blake Hobi

[13]I know one of the other suspects, and we sometimes play catch with a football in his backyard.

Bryan Knutson

[14]I know two of the other suspects, and I played football with one of them every year through our graduation year. [15]None of us would ever steal from a family.

The Innocent

Use complete sentences and sentence numbers to describe the best evidence for your conclusions.

______________________________ (suspect name)

____

____

____

____

______________________________ (suspect name)

____

____

____

____

______________________________ (suspect name)

____

____

____

____

The Football Thief

______________________________ (suspect name)

____

____

____

____

Read the mystery below to find evidence to identify the innocent and guilty suspects. Remember, the story and suspects' statements are true.

The Coffee Mug Thief

[1]Today, police in the City of Bandon arrested one of the four women shown below for stealing an expensive coffee mug from Nelson's Coffee shop. [2]The theft took place on Monday, June 7, between 8 a.m. and 9 a.m. [3]All four suspects were in the store during that time. [4]The owner said he remembered that O'Bryan and Nicolaus bought coffee and that Nicolaus had chatted with Giss around 8:45 a.m. [5]Giss said she didn't buy anything in the store, but saw a woman in a blue or green top put something in her purse. [6]O'Bryan said she doesn't drink coffee and was just in the store getting things for her husband. [7]A witness in the store at the time of the theft said he didn't see the theft, but the person he suspected had dark hair and was wearing a dark skirt. [8]He also told police that Giss left the store with Nicolaus before Smith and O'Bryan.

[9]The police arrived a few minutes after 9 a.m. the day of theft and then questioned each suspect in her nearby residence. [10]The arrest of the suspect and her later confession happened shortly after. [11]The mug was found in one of the residences and returned to the store.

Laurie Smith

[12]I bought coffee in the store today, and we have plenty of coffee mugs at home, so I don't have to steal coffee mugs. [13]I wasn't the last suspect to leave the store.

Carrie O'Bryan

[14]I looked at the mug and even put it in my open purse to buy it, but I later decided it wasn't worth the price and put it back just before leaving the store.

Michelle Nicolaus

[15]I was with my friend Robin as soon as she entered the store until the time we left. [16]She didn't have a chance to steal the mug when I was with her.

Robin Giss

[17]I did pick the mug up and look at it, but I thought it was too expensive for my taste. [18]Michelle thought it was ugly and didn't go near it after I looked at it.

The Innocent

Use complete sentences and sentence numbers to describe the best evidence for your conclusions.

______________________________ (suspect name)

____

____

____

____

______________________________ (suspect name)

____

____

____

____

______________________________ (suspect name)

____

____

____

____

The Coffee Mug Thief

______________________________ (suspect name)

____

____

____

____

Answers

The Car Thief (p. 2-3)

The Innocent

Jake Smith: Sentence 6 states that the thief was six feet or slightly taller, and in sentence 11, Trey Woods says all of them are about six feet tall. Looking at the picture, Jake Smith is clearly short of six feet tall, so he is not the thief. Sentence 6 also states that the thief had dark pants and Jake Smith has light pants. This eliminates Jake Smith.

Ben Daily: Sentence 6 states that the thief was six feet or slightly taller, and in sentence 11, Trey Woods said all of them are about six feet tall. Looking at the picture, Ben Daily is clearly short of six feet tall. This eliminates Ben Daily.

Trey Woods: Sentence 5 states that the witness said he saw just a lone young man break into the car and drive away. In sentence 10, Trey Woods says he was always with his two friends. This eliminates Trey Woods.

The Car Thief

Bill Lucero: Lucero is the car thief because the other three suspects can be proven innocent, and sentence 1 states that one of the four boys was arrested and confessed to the crime. There was no evidence that Lucero did not steal the car.

The Lunch Money Thief (p. 4-5)

The Innocent

Jodi Morgan: In sentence 15, Morgan says that she has never had anything to do with Clemens, so she could not have taken her money. If you take someone's money, then you have had something to do with them. This eliminates Jodi Morgan.

Jane Mott: In sentence 10, Mott says that she entered the cafeteria with 20 dollars. In sentence in 17, she says that she never had someone else's money in the cafeteria. This eliminates Jane Mott.

Susan Ueberrhein: In sentence 11, Ueberrhein says that she left the counter with the same amount of money she had when she entered the cafeteria. In sentence 18, she says that she didn't buy anything or spend any money. If she had, she would have left the counter with less money. This eliminates Susan Ueberrhein.

The Lunch Money Thief

Deanna Edwards: Edwards is the lunch money thief because the other three suspects can be proven innocent, and sentence 13 states that one of the suspects was the thief. In sentence 8, Edwards says that she left the cafeteria with less than five dollars. Also, in sentence 14, she says that she paid for her lunch with money out of her pocket, but we don't know how that money got in her pocket, how much money she entered the cafeteria with, or how much money she spent.

The Chicken Breast Thief (p. 6-7)

The Innocent

Leonard: In sentence 13, Scott Jacobsen says that the cat he saw with the chicken breast in his mouth had a light gray neck. This eliminates Leonard.

Betty: In sentence 14, Ellie Jacobsen says that she saw the cat with the chicken breast and it had two light gray legs. This eliminates Betty.

Chipper: In sentences 16 and 17, Richard Litts says he saw the cat with the chicken breast and that it had pointed ears. This eliminates Chipper.

The Chicken Breast Thief

Rudolf: Rudolf is the chicken breast thief because the other three suspects can be proven innocent, and Rudolf fits the descriptions of all the witnesses except for Kathy Litts'. Kathy's description, in sentence 10, is not very important since the cat she saw was in the "front yard," not the backyard where the chicken breast was taken. Also, the cat she saw in the front yard was not seen with the chicken breast.

The Necklace Thief (p. 8-9)

The Innocent

Shannon Porter: In sentence 13, Porter says that she left the necklace on the counter before the theft and never had it again. This eliminates Shannon Porter.

Terri Collier: In sentence 9, the witness states that the thief asked the owner a question before the theft. Sentence 12 identifies the owner as a woman. In sentences 14 and 15, Collier says she asked the man who was helping a question about the necklace and didn't speak to anyone else. This eliminates Terri Collier.

Mindy Smith: In sentence 9, the witness states that the thief asked the owner a question before the theft. Sentence 12 identifies the owner as a woman. In sentences 16 and 17, Smith says she was waited on by a young man and that he was the only person she talked to before 5 p.m., and the theft occurred between 3 p.m. and 5 p.m. This eliminates Mindy Smith.

The Necklace Thief

Miriam Zomerschoe: Zomerschoe is the necklace thief because the other three suspects can be proven innocent, and sentence 11 states that one of the four suspects was the thief. In sentence 9, the witness states that the thief asked the owner a question before the theft; in sentence 18, Zomerschoe says that she did speak with a woman in the store just after 4 p.m., and the theft took place between 3 p.m. and 5 p.m.

The Bath Robe Thief (p. 10-11)

The Innocent

Darin O'Bryan: Sentence 11 states that stolen robe was found in the thief's apartment. In sentence 14, O'Bryan says that the stolen robe was never in his apartment. This eliminates Darin O'Bryan.

John Nicolaus: Sentence 11 states that the stolen robe was blue and white, and in sentences 15 and 16, Nicolaus says he left the store with items that were partly green. An object that is all blue and white cannot also be partly green. This eliminates John Nicolaus.

Steve Giss: Sentence 11 states that stolen robe was found in the thief's apartment. In sentence 17, Giss says he was on the way to his house. This eliminates Steve Giss.

The Bath Robe Thief

Michael Baker: Baker is the bath robe thief because the other three suspects can be proven innocent, and sentence 10 states that one of the four suspects was arrested and confessed. In sentence 8, the witness states that the suspect was short, and Michael Baker is shorter than two of the other suspects, but we cannot tell from the picture the height of any of the suspects. For example, it could be that all of the suspects are short.

The Big City Bicycle Thief (p. 12-13)

The Innocent

Sam Edwards: In sentence 9, Witness 2 says that the thief had a large, red scar across his cheek. Edwards does not have a scar in the picture. This eliminates Sam Edwards.

Steve Berta: In sentence 15, Berta says that when he left the phone store he went "straight home," and in sentence 16 he says that on his journey home, he looked back and saw the bicycle in front of the store. If he had left for home, and went straight home, and at one point looked back and saw the bicycle, then he couldn't have taken the bicycle nor turned around to go back and get it. This eliminates Steve Berta.

Kent Kitchel: In sentence 10, Witness 3 says that the thief had dark facial hair. Kitchel does not have any facial hair in the picture. This eliminates Kent Kitchel.

The Big City Bicycle Thief

Bob Veach: Veach is the bicycle thief because the other three suspects can be proven innocent, and sentences 1 and 5 state one of the four suspects was arrested and confessed the theft. There is also no evidence that Veach did not steal the bicycle.

The Purse Thief (p. 14-15)

The Innocent

Bonnie Baker: Sentences 4, 5, and 6 state that the theft occurred in the second half between the 2nd and 3rd goals of the game. In sentence 11, Baker says that she was not at the game in the second half. This eliminates Baker.

Mary O'Dell: Sentences 4, 5, and 6 state that the theft occurred in the second half between the 2nd and the 3rd goals of the game. Sentence 10 states that the final score of the game was 3–1, and in sentence 12 Mary says she arrived at the game for the final goal, so she was not at the game when the theft occurred between the 2nd and 3rd goals. This eliminates O'Dell.

Jessica Garrett: In sentence 9, the witness states that the thief had darkish hair, and Jessica's hair isn't very dark in the picture. The best evidence is sentence 15; Jessica says that she was not at the game during the 2nd and 3rd goals. Sentences 4, 5, and 6 state that the theft occurred in the second half between the 2nd and 3rd goals of the game. Jessica had left in the second half before the 1st goal of the second half was scored, so she left the game after the 1st goal and before the 2nd and 3rd goals, when the theft occurred. This eliminates Garrett.

The Purse Thief

Jacqueline Examilotis: Examilotis is the purse thief because the other three suspects can be proven innocent, and sentences 1 and 10 state that one of the four suspects was arrested for the crime and confessed.

The Plant Thief (p. 16-17)

The Innocent

Jorge Sanchez: In sentence 13, Sanchez says that he never thought of taking the plant. If you never thought of taking something, then you couldn't take it. This eliminates Jorge Sanchez.

Steve Krauth: Sentence 6 states that the plant was not stolen until after 11:10 a.m. In sentence 15, Krauth says he didn't go near it after 11 a.m. This eliminates Steve Krauth.

Jeff Cort: In sentence 17, Cort says that he wanted to buy it but thought it was sold when it was no longer in the pot. If it was no longer in the pot, then the thief had already stolen it. This eliminates Jeff Court.

The Plant Thief

Ross Wilson: Wilson is the plant thief because the other three suspects can be proven innocent, and sentence 11 states that one of the four suspects was arrested and confessed to the crime. In sentence 12, Wilson says that he knows who took the plant, but this doesn't tell us much, since we don't know what the meaning of "know" is in this sentence. Even if he has knowledge of who did it, it does not eliminate himself.

The Dog Food Thief (p. 18-19)

The Innocent

Ralph: Sentence 7 states that the last theft occurred in the morning, and in sentence 13 Ralph's owner said Ralph is only out of his pen in the afternoon. This eliminates Ralph.

Toby: In sentence 14, Toby's owner says Toby can only go to the Ortega's Mondays, Thursdays, and Saturdays, and sentence 6 states the second theft was on the 9th, which was a Wednesday. This eliminates Toby.

Shadow: In sentence 15, Shadow's owner says that Shadow is female, and sentence 12 states that the thief is a male. This eliminates Shadow.

The Dog Food Thief

Pepper: Pepper is the dog food thief because the other three suspects can be proven innocent, and sentence 10 states that Pepper is a male dog, since Mr. Ortega calls Pepper and Ralph the hairy brothers. Sentence 12 states that the thief is a male.

The Tie Thief (p. 20-21)

The Innocent

Tyler Morgan: In sentence 5, the owner states that the thief is one of the store's best buying customers, and in sentence 10, Morgan says that he has only bought one thing from the store and returned it. This eliminates Tyler Morgan.

Don Tedsen: In sentence 13, Slivkoff says that he was shocked when the police made their arrest and in sentence 14, he says that nothing Tedsen has done has ever surprised him. If Tedsen has never surprised him, then Tedsen is not the thief. This eliminates Don Tedsen.

Steve Slivkoff: In sentence 14, Slivkoff says that he has known Tedsen a long time and in sentences 15 and 16, Tedsen says that he knows two of the suspects, but only one suspect for a long time. That suspect would have to be Slivkoff and in sentence 17, Tedsen says that that friend (Slivkoff) did not take the ties. This eliminates Steve Slivkoff.

The Tie Thief

Ralph Smith: Smith is the tie thief because the other suspects can be proven innocent, and sentence 3 states that one of the suspects was arrested. There also is no evidence that Smith did not steal the ties.

The Football Thief (p. 22-23)

The Innocent

Norm Day: In sentence 10, Day says that the last football he has seen was on Sunday. Sentence 1 states that the football was stolen on Saturday and sentence 6 states that the suspects' statements were given on the day of the crime, so Day did not see a football on the day of the theft. Also, in sentence 14, Knutson says that he knows two of the suspects, and that he played football with one of them through their graduation year. In sentence 11, Meizner says that he was cut from his high school football team as a senior, so Knutson's two friends are Day and Hobi. In sentence 15, Knutson says that he, Hobi, and Day would never steal from a family, and sentence 2 states that the Bakers are a family. This eliminates Norm Day.

Bryan Knutson: In sentence 14, Knutson says that he knows two of the suspects, and that he played football with one of them through their graduation year. In sentence 11, Meizner says that he was cut from his high school football team as a senior, so Knutson's two friends are Day and Hobi. In sentence 15, Knutson says that he, Hobi, and Day would never steal from a family, and sentence 2 tells us the Bakers are a family. This eliminates Bryan Knutson.

Blake Hobi: In sentence 14, Knutson says that he knows two of the suspects, and that he played football with one of them through their graduation year. In sentence 11, Meizner says that he was cut from his high school football team as a senior, so Knutson's two friends are Day and Hobi. In sentence 15, Knutson says that he, Hobi, and Day would never steal from a family, and sentence 2 tells us the Bakers are a family. This eliminates Blake Hobi.

The Football Thief

Kyle Meizner: Meizner is the football thief because the other suspects can be proven innocent, and sentences 8 and 9 state that one of the suspects was arrested and confessed to the crime. There also is no evidence that Meizner did not steal the football.

The Coffee Mug Thief (p. 24-25)

The Innocent

Carrie O'Bryan: In sentence 14, O'Bryan says that she put the coffee mug back "just before leaving the store." This eliminates Carrie O'Bryan.

Michelle Nicolaus: In sentence 18, Giss says that Nicolaus never went near the mug after she (Giss) looked at it. If Nicolaus never went near the mug after Giss looked at it, then Nicolaus could not have stolen the mug. This eliminates Michelle Nicolaus.

Robin Giss: In sentence 15, Nicolaus says she was with Giss from the time she entered the store to the time they left. In sentence 16, Nicolaus says that Giss never had a chance to steal the mug when she was with her which would have been Giss's entire time in the store. This eliminates Robin Giss.

The Coffee Mug Thief

Laurie Smith: Smith is the coffee mug thief because the other three suspects can be proven innocent, and sentences 1, 10, and 11 state that the police arrested one of the four suspects, the suspect confessed to the crime, and the stolen mug was found at the thief's residence. There is also no evidence to prove Smith's innocence. In sentence 13, Smith says that she was not the last to leave the store, but that doesn't prove anything about the theft.